Some pencil marks

AF711018

Hear The Music!

A New Approach To Mental Health

Norman E. Hoffman

Star Publishing Company, Inc.
Boynton Beach, Fla.

$4.95

FIRST PRINTING – OCTOBER 1974

Cover Design Created By
Judie

COPYRIGHT © 1974 BY NORMAN HOFFMAN
ALL RIGHTS RESERVED.
NO PART OF THIS BOOK MAY BE REPRODUCED IN ANY FORM
WITHOUT PERMISSION IN WRITING FROM THE AUTHOR.

PRINTED IN THE UNITED STATES OF AMERICA
BY STAR PUBLISHING COMPANY, INC., BOYNTON BEACH, FLORIDA

LIBRARY OF CONGRESS CARD NUMBER: 74–25052

Dedicated to

J, J & J

I would like to express my deep appreciation to Robert Alsofrom, Ph.D. and to Peter Herschman, M.D. for their many hours of editing, consultation and interest in my work. I would also like to thank Alan Levine, M.D., George Blanck and the Community Mental Health Center of Palm Beach County for their interest and encouragement in my research project in helping develop the Hoffman Test for Organicity. In addition I would like to thank a good friend Grace and my dedicated wife Judie.

In a very special acknowledgement I would like to express my most sincere gratitude and appreciation to a remarkable woman, Florence Dix Kronsky. Without her constant support and unselfish dedication to my beliefs and theories in music therapy, this book would not have been possible.

I consider the opportunity to inscribe this brief preface to Dr. Hoffman's book as a distinct privilege. After observing therapeutic techniques come and go for twenty five years, I look upon works which claim to break new ground with a great deal of reservations. Most of them turn out to be rediscoveries of the wheel under a new name. In comparison, Dr. Hoffman does indeed present a new and genuinely effective therapeutic vehicle.

This work is the logical result of original investigations in the field of Music Therapy. It should be regarded as basic — the first systematic approach based on innovative but experimentally sound investigation, as well as brilliant observation.

Those of my colleagues who have struggled with varying degrees of discouragement, sometimes verging on despair, to establish some type of therapeutic communication with those who will not respond — the withdrawn, the autistic, the depressed — will share my deep appreciation for the technique delineated in this volume. I think any experienced therapist can almost literally reach back into his past and pick out a particularly recalcitrant non-responder and know that this technique would have worked with that case had it been available.

I hope to see music therapy widely practiced in the near future and I believe this book will stimulate its general acceptance. The successful therapeuses which I confidently predict will result where there was only stalemate or failure before, will explain my sense of privilege in being associated in however small a way with Dr. Hoffman's work.

Robert K. Alsofrom, Ph.D.

Chapter I

Brief History of Music Therapy

Musical history is complex and parallels the cognitive and emotional development of man. The earliest known records of men living in groups associate music and magic. Great powers were ascribed to the Shaman, or medicine man, whose procedures frequently were accompanied by music. In time, music attained symbolic aspects, emblematic of his control of the spirits.(1) Often it became a direct tool of treatment. Primitive men believed melody could exorcise evil spirits and even heal wounds.(2)

David calmed and soothed Saul by playing his harp, easing his affliction and removing the evil spirits which tormented him.

Pythagorus believed that musical sounds, prescribed daily could contribute effectively to health maintenance.(3) Plato linked music to the moral welfare of the entire nation, because he thought the soul could lose its harmony, thus causing discontent. Melody and rhythm, he felt, could be used as a means of restoring the soul to order and concord. He reasoned, by changing the musical note, the foundations of the state could be undermined.(4) Music became influential in altering public morals; an ethical consideration evolved. Different Greek musical modes were assigned an area of influence on personality; i.e., Lydian was decorous and educative, Phrygian violent and emotional, Dorian composed and manly.(5)

Martin Luther believed music could exorcise the devil and other evil spirits.(6)

During the seventeenth century a specific disease, Tarantism, was treated by music. Many individuals in the heat-stricken town of Apulia, Italy, suddenly jumped from their homes to dance and run about with frenzied excitement. Some people collapsed and several died until the controlling effective music was recognized. The tarantella evolved, so named due to popular belief that the spider caused the malady. The fast tempo, frequently repeated, was soon regarded as a cure for this apparently hysterical social phenomenon.(7)

For many years music was left to religious and mystical experiences with neglect of its therapeutic benefits; but then, during the eighteenth and nineteenth centuries, many began to look for a more scientific method of utilizing music in the treatment of mental disorders.

Not until 1926 was music used definitively as a portion of the therapeutic milieu. The music was provided generally voluntarily, by every type of organization — instrumental and vocal soloists, orchestras, choruses and musical comedy troupes. Staff members at all levels contributed their services.(8)

Music became more developed to existing treatments such as physio, psycho and occupational therapies, to accompany physical exercises, and facilitate socialization. Its first professional recognition as a therapeutic tool emerged among occupational therapists.(9)

Introduced into hospital programs in an uncertain manner, music was not integrated into therapeutic programs. Certainly, there was general lack of awareness of its use and power. The staff member of a hospital in charge of music was given no recognition as a regular therapist, being left on his own to include music in the on-going therapeutic programs. His efforts, understandably, were often blundering and ineffective. He received no professional respect, and was often regarded as a "character." His observations of the patient's reaction to music, no matter how perceptive and relevant to the patient's condition or progress, were not included in the regular progress reports or explored in staff conferences. He was able to function unimpeded by staying out of the way of other hospital personnel.

Van de Wall held a pioneering attitude for the position and practice of the hospital musician: "The general objective of any hospital music program is to provide the patient with pleasurable musical experiences of a comforting and encouraging nature. This implies that all hospital music activities should be selected and performed in a way to invite the interest and active participation of the patients.(10)

Any newly appointed music worker should be given ample opportunity to observe and learn to recognize attitudes and methods of other staff members in their dealings with various types of patients. Understanding the attitudes and methods of his fellow workers, besides some of their problems, and their need for cooperative support by other staff members will help the musician to see where he is with his specialty, where he may become a collaborator and also wherein lies the limits of his particular approach.(11)

The benefits to be derived from the application of music as a measure of hospital treatment are conditioned, as we have seen, by four interactive factors; a recognition of and administration provision for well-regulated music services within the hospital organization; the presence of physicians and other staff members who make use of the music facilities of the hospital according to the same principles of accuracy that they apply to the other forms and methods of treatment; the qualities of music as a stimulus and incentive of medically and culturally desirable physiopsychological and social functioning; the qualifications of musicians rendering service to the hospitals.(12)

Clinical experience indicates that the mood of psychotic patients can be influenced if a special musical technique is employed. Slow, sad music will capture the mood of a depressed patient. Fast, exciting music reaches the manic. Only after the music therapist has aligned himself through the appropriate musical approach with the patient's mood, can a shift to a different mood, through a different tempo or musical quality be made.(13) Therapists recognize that active participation is a more potent factor in influencing patient mood and behavior than passive listening to radio, phonograph, and motion picture sound reels. Such activity varies according to the musical abilities of the patient and many include group or choir singing, rhythm bands, musical games, auto-harps, and dancing.

The active application of music to the patient's life has special advantages; it stimulates actual intellectual involvement in the activity and can produce ego-satisfaction and enhancement or self-respect through a self-judged successful performance; it arouses emotionality and then provides an outlet for its expression; and it is also a possible cooperative group action.

Full recognition of the value of music as a productive therapeutic technique and the need for trained music specialists in hospitals, led to the organization of the National Association of Music Therapy in 1950. From its inception, the association has been committed to "progressive development of the use of music in medicine, and the advancement of research, interests and standards in music therapy." (Schneider) (14)

Chapter II

Training, Experience, Recognition

Although the historical approach serves as a useful introduction to basic concepts of music therapy, recently more scientific explorations germinated significant results.

In 1965 the U.S. Department of Health, Education and Welfare supported a cooperative research program in music therapy. The principal participants in the project, headed by E. Thayer Gaston of the University of Kansas, were teachers of music therapy in colleges and universities who held advanced degrees, and who were registered music therapists with the National Association for Music Therapy.

Schneider, past president of the N.A.M.T. states in the introduction: The challenge of some psychiatrists forced music therapists to examine their procedures and achievements more closely. Other psychiatrists were content, in fact insisted, in regarding music as an activity only.

Examinations of practices and accomplishments made it apparent that music therapists needed to know more about man and his responses to music. It became evident that mere performance was not sufficient to put a patient into better condition. No longer was it enough for the music therapist merely to play music for the patients. Music therapists had to pay more attention to the nature of man; they had to learn more about him.(15)

Schneider was concerned with developing sufficiently adequate training for the music therapist to make him worthy of the title. He should, through thorough and relevant preparation, be able to genuinely treat a patient, not merely entertain him.

In part I (Gaston) "Man and Music" it says: Music is human behavior. This short statement provides the thesis, not only of this chapter, but of those which follow. Very simply, it means that we are concerned primarily with human beings, with the many ways they are influenced by music.(16) Gaston presents music therapy as a behavioral science in a logical, cogent discussion. He makes a strong case for the need of its proponents to constantly inform themselves of the latest achievements and researches in the established behavioral sciences, in addition to studying music with whatever scientific precision is possible, as it related to man's behavior.

In Part 2, Sears describes the need for an objective approach to music processes which he categorizes as a behavioral science aimed at a progressive development of music therapy.(17)

The remainder of his resume (parts 3 to 9) could serve as a general introduction to the subject for the music therapy student.

TRAINING:

The music therapist must be equipped with a sound knowledge of both music and psychological processes before attempting to interweave the two in music therapy.

He must, in the musical area, be able to improvise modes, harmonies, rhythms, tempo and meter with the absolute freedom of professional mastery of music theory. All of these aspects of music are constantly brought into play as he finds himself involved with the many different personality difficulties encountered in a psychotherapeutic practice.

In the psychological area, he must have the usual requisite skills of any trained therapist — the experience and theoretical background to establish or re-establish interpersonal relationships, strengthen impaired or weakened ego functions, create suitable rapport with a variety of personalities, etc. Music therapy is considered applicable to patients of all ages, from early childhood to those suffering from geriatric difficulties. Music therapy. therefore, may be equated in its techniques and goals, with any other type of psychotherapy. It commences with the deliberate creation of a relationship between the therapist and the patients for the desired modification of the patient's behavior. As it is now used in the institutional setting, music therapy is multifaceted. It explores, in order to better diagnose or define for future therapeutic advance, various patterns of disturbed behavior. It tries to remove, modify or retard existing symptoms so that positive personality growth and development may be obtained, along with a more effective way of handling a variety of life problems.(18)

EXPERIENCE

It is perhaps belaboring the obvious to note that no psychotherapist can become genuinely competent and effective in his efforts without adequate experience. If music therapy is to gain credibility, and take on a responsible professional stature, then each person claiming the title must have the same predictable background of exposure to the cases he will be expected to deal with as his opposite numbers in all of the allied licensed healing professions.

His experience, at the professional level, must consist of, in addition to the prescribed didactic material, supervised experience at increasingly responsible levels with his prospective patients. Strict standards must be set, in addition, for those who assume the task of the supervision. These persons, indeed, must be selected with far more care than the students.

The emphasis, other than the formal information contained in the psychiatric and psychological courses, is on the thorough study and preparation of the case history. It is of paramount importance for the music therapist trainee to use such histories constructively, to understand the relevance and propriety of applying his resources to a case, and to construct from them a well ordered therapeutic strategy. Examples of the type and structure of such case histories will be given in Chap. VI.

RECOGNITION

Because of its recent arrival on the therapeutic scene, there is much confusion concerning the role of the therapy and the capabilities of the therapist representing it. The author feels this is a constant present responsibility, to carefully and explicitly explain both to the general lay and professional public. He feels in addition, that this responsibility must be gracefully but determinedly assumed by all concerned members of the profession. General professional acceptance and status as a recognized therapeutic technique cannot just happen — they have to be earned by the most solicitous attention to the standards set for practice, the levels of proficiency to be attained by each aspiring trainee, and a dignified but resolute leadership from the national professional societies.

The problem of professional acceptance, and status as understood by allied therapeutic professions probably had its inception in the late 1940 when Karl Menninger attempted to organize the various activity therapies. Attempting to relate them to the order of mental hospital function, he coined the term "adjunctive therapist" to describe the proponents of recreational and occupational therapies and how they stood vis-a-vis the pyschiatic and psychological, mainly the latter. It clearly deposited major responsibility for the case in the hands of the medical man.(19)

Just as clearly he implied there were distinct differences in training and philosophy among the various therapies. Rather than clear things up, it raised even more vexing questions. Are such therapists lay or professional people — a distinction which makes vast differences in their authority, their fees, their acceptance by health insurance companies, and their status in the pecking order of a hospital staff.

The author wishes to take a definite stand in favor of regarding the music therapist as a professional, who, when properly trained and experienced, is fully capable of taking his place in the treatment of the mentally troubled as an independent practitioner. As a member of a professional team, capable of extending opinions sufficiently expert and authoritative, he should be accepted as co-equal in force with any other member.

The functions of the psychologist and psychiatrist are widely and instantly recognized by both laymen and professionals. The music therapist, however, claims that, particularly in the examination-evaluation field, where the vital information is derived from the patient as to the appropriate diagnosis and consequent treatment course, the tests and techniques applied by these two professions are so often so vague and inconclusive that the choice of therapeutic procedure remains little more than an intuitive inspiration. The music therapist claims that he can reach many of these individuals with a type of communication unavailable to other professions and is able to derive significant and reliable information from them, available in no other way. This information may be used appropriately by the other professions if any diagnostic consultation is used; however, the music therapist maintains that some of the types of cases which respond to this mode of communication are also treatable by no other method as effectively, or at all, as by music therapy. He, therefore, claims that music therapy in selected instances is an entity of treatment and should be so regarded, when the resources of the treatment team are canvassed for proper therapeutic strategies.

Here it seems necessary to make the point strongly that the role of the music therapist differs markedly from that of the music educator. The latter is essentially an instructor. His main purpose is to provide formal training in a variety of musical skills. Such a description obviously limits him to being a teacher. For the music therapist, however, music becomes a tool for behavioral change, not an end skill to be achieved for itself. It can be used to reach and help the emotional disturbances of even severely mentally ill human beings. Many of them display the isolation, self-enclosure, inarticulateness and lack of motivation to respond, which are the despair of many therapists adhering to other, older methods. For many of them, musical expression has proved to be their single communicative link with the rest of the human community.

Unfortunately, the status of music therapy as a credible promulgator of such claims is still substantially in doubt. Many of its practitioners cry for recognition of music therapy as a behavioral science and an independent profession, yet, there has been a sad failure on the part of the professionals in the field of music therapy to assist in achieving this recognition. Confusion has been confounded by their persistent unwillingness or inability to make clear, valid, believable distinctions between music for the purposes of teaching and music as a tool for treatment. It is essential that the music therapist be able to collaborate with psychiatrists and psychologist on an independent professional level.

Professional status can only be achieved when the music therapist is subject to a training program equivalent in depth to his clinical colleagues. We must expand our resources to do so. The effective practice of competent music therapists who have asserted their new behavioral techniques and used them in effective treatment programs have been given individual recognition and concomitant professional status as qualified therapists. It is clearly the ever present responsibility of the professional leadership of the music therapy profession to take a strong, active lead in creating the training programs, the professional standards and goals which will produce respect for the competence of the newly arrived members of the profession.

Appendix
Chapter II

The following is a training program for interns in music therapy. It is designed to extend for one year. As will be noted, it combines a specialized supervised clinical format of seminars, conferences and case discussions, with the customary formal diadactic efforts of the psychiatric department of a medical school. The program is based on work with all degrees of pathology. The training is to be divided into three phases. Part I would include:

a — *Clinical Observation* — Supervised trainees make daily observations in selected classrooms and during recreational periods on preselected children whose behavior has been diagnosed as early pathological disturbance of various types.

b — *Case studies* — Trainees will be required to submit brief summarizing reports of their observations, incorporating background clinical material made available from hospital files. Deciding on the type and possible etiology of the observed disturbance will be emphasized.

c — *Seminar on early childhood psychoses* — Here the trainee will be introduced to the diagnoses, clinical observations, and therapeutic methods relating to such conditions as infantile autism, anaclitic depression, and other manifestations of childhood schizophrenia.

d — *Seminar on therapeutic principles of childrens' psychotherapy* — This will involve introducing the trainee to the principles of play therapy, childrens' psychoanalysis and behavior therapy for children.

e — *Seminar on improvisational skills* — The trainee will be exposed to improvisational techniques, often quite spontaneous, which occur regularly in professional music therapy sessions through the media of television and sound tapes. To be conducted by a music therapist.

Part II would include:

a — *Clinical observations* — Continuation of procedures learned in the first phase with emphasis on sharpening and refining observational techniques.

b — *Individual case study* — Trainee will be assigned a specific child to observe and evaluate. The study would be detailed on social and physical history, trainee's observations, relevant background information from the psychologist and psychiatrist. His own therapeutic program would necessarily evolve from his evaluation.

c — *Seminar on early childhood development* — This would include the available observations on the social, psychological and physical developmental stages from infancy to six years. To be conducted jointly by a psychiatrist and a pediatrician.

d — *Exploratory evaluation of music therapy* — A discussion of the skills necessary in the initial observational and treatment phases of music therapy. To be conducted by a music therapist.

e — *Seminar on improvisational skills* — The trainee will be exposed to improvisational techniques, often quite spontaneous, which occur regularly in professional music therapy sessions through the media of television and sound tapes. To be conducted by a music therapist.

f — *Observations of group music therapy* — Regular (at least bi-weekly) observation of group music therapy sessions with emphasis on learning how to establish interpersonal relationships between the therapist and the group members, and with each other in a supportive, non-threatening situation.

Part III would include:

a — *Supervised experience in individual music therapy* — The trainee will be given opportunities for active participation in therapy sessions, with attention to both verbal and non-verbal patients. To be supervised by a music therapist.

b — *Seminar on group therapy* — Basic concepts and techniques of group psychotherapy will be discussed, particularly the role of the group leader. To be conducted by all regular members of the hospital group therapy team.

c —*Supervised experience in group therapy* — The trainees will participate in active group therapy sessions involving play and relationship therapies. They will meet with both early childhood schizophrenias, and be introduced to adolescent psychotics. To be conducted by members of the hospital therapy team including a music therapist.

d — *Terminal reports* — Trainees will be required to submit terminal reports on assigned cases. These reports will consist of final clinical observations of individual cases under study, final summaries of therapy sessions, recommendations and conclusions for the individual cases studied.

Trainees will also submit evaluations of their personal and professional experiences during the training program. These will be used by the supervisory staff of music therapists to improve future training programs.

Chapter III

"But I'm Not Rhythmic"

Rhythm is an integral part of the entire life process. It exists in every human being; for he breathes in rhythm and walks in rhythm. His entire circulatory system functions rhythmically.

But what happens when an individual cannot perceive rhythm or does not have the capacity to perceive rhythmic patterns? What happens when there is a dysfunction in any one of the many bodily rhythmic functions, i.e., heartbeat, breathing, walking, talking, etc.? Is it not true that whenever any one of these bodily rhythmic functions is impaired, there is a resulting disability in one's daily life style to some degree?

Although Freud explicity called attention to the importance of rhythmicity nearly 60 years ago, it remained one of the most neglected aspects of infant activity in psychoanalytic research. While more research in this area is definitely needed, we do know some startling facts. It has been shown that rhythmicity begins in the neonatal stage of development.

The following summary of fetal development is based on the study of surgically separated fetuses.(21)

The beginning of heartbeat, life's most basic rhythm, occurs in the third week when the embryo is only about 4mm. in length. By the sixth week a spontaneous, wormlike movement of the arms, legs, and trunk has been observed. By the third month spontaneous movements of a slow, uncoordinated type appear. The sum total of responses during the latter part of this period involves movement at every joint. The rhythm of respiratory movements have also been noted near the close of this period. By the fifth month, generalized body activity has so increased in intensity that the average mother has no difficulty in reporting strong fetal movements. Hiccups have been observed in the fetus during this period, occurring about fifteen to thirty times a minute. Rhythmic sucking reflexes can be evoked by tactile stimulation of the oral region in the sixth month. Almost all of the responses that can be evoked from the normal newborn can be elicited during the seventh month.

In one investigation, fetal heartbeat was studied during the last six months of pregnancy by stethoscopic observation. It was found that fetal heartbeat increased somewhat after the mother had smoked a cigarette and that a vibratory stimulus applied to the mother's abdomen near the position of the fetus' head produced an increase of heartbeat approximately ten beats per minute during the last two months of fetal life.

It has been demonstrated that a variety of sounds (buzzers, bells, etc.) may evoke an increase in fetal activity during and after the 31st week of pregnancy.

A non classic case of fetal activity in response to sound (or vibration) stimulation was reported. Approximately one month before her baby was born, a mother was bathing in a metal tub. When one of her children, playing in the bathroom, accidentally struck the side of the tub with a glass jar, the fetus responded with a sudden jump. The mother reported that she felt no vibration transmitted through the water. A deliberate repetition of the experience a few days later provided the same results.

The heartbeat of the fetus during the fifth month of pregnancy is approximately 150 to 155 beats per minute;

the rate gradually decreases during the remainder of the fetal period so that an average rate of 130 beats per minute is observed at the time of birth. It is interesting to note that the rate of heartbeat declines rather sharply during the first two years of postnatal life and then continues a less precipitous decline with further development until an average of approximately eighty beats per minute is observed in mature individuals.

These rhythmic patterns beginning with life itself are taken for granted; and yet, perhaps rhythmic dysfunction in later years could possibly result from interruption of these normal rhythmic developmental stages. Certainly, much more research is needed in this area.

After birth the baby's rhythmic development is more easily observed. Spitz mentions that the rhythm of the closing and the opening of the baby's hand around the mother's finger is in some way related to the rhythm of his sucking. How this coordination may relate to rhythm emerging at a later stage is yet unexplored.

As one baby bangs his head against the bed, another rolls it from side to side. Still another gets up on his hands and knees and rhythmically jounces down against his heels. What is the meaning of these rhythmic movements? I don't think we know for sure.

As far back as 1936 Van de Wall noted the importance of rhythm in childhood. He said, "In the preschool and kindergarten age, a period of rapid physical growth, the child has great need for sensorially pleasing experiences; for impressions that encourage rather than frighten him and that give feelings of confidence and security; and for activity that uses his whole body and not alone his arms and legs. He lives in the present, hence what happens to him and what he can do at the moment have great significance. He is attracted by relatively soft rather than loud sounds, and by simple, clear rhythms. His span of attention and concentration is short; his feelings and ideas are few; his expression is simple in form and brief in duration. The music that best fits such capabilities consists of short tunes with simple words that have a meaning for the child — melodies in a small tonal range which he can easily sing. He loves to jump and run and execute little dances. The dances taught him should be brief and consist of a few figures of simple movements. His rhythmic reactions to sound being rather pronounced, at a very early age he enjoys beating rhythmic orchestra instruments."

Van de Wall also says that 'Children of the sense and motor-training group, below four years mentally and ten years chronologically, are encouraged to identify among other sense impression sounds such as those from bells, horns, and whistles. They love to respond to drums by bodily motion and can be taught to do simple rhythm work like beating with sticks and marching to musical trains.' He goes on to say, 'Children from five to twelve years chronologically, and from four to five and one-half years mentally, are assigned to the kindergarten class. Many show keen interest in rhythm orchestra work. The flexibility of their rhythmic response increases with a higher intelligence.(30)

We have discussed the importance of rhythmicity in the developing child. Now we must turn our attention to the pathological symptoms that arise when the normal developmental stages and patterns are interrupted by circumstances in the environment. Furthermore, we must examine how some of these pathological symptoms result in a rhythmic dysfunction.

In Spitz's research with children who rock

pathologically he concluded that the relation between the rocking children and their mother was a peculiar one. He felt that their babies were exposed alternately to intense outbursts of fondling of 'love' and to equally intense outbursts of hostility and rage.(31) He goes to state that in normal development the infant would proceed through successive stages leading to the establishment of the libidinal object. But in rocking children, the mother has stunted the establishment of the primal, of the libidinal object and thereby made all object relations difficult or impossible for the child.(32) The child's normal object formation being disturbed, thumb sucking, playing with the lips, ears, nose, hair, etc., goes to the objectless activity or rocking. This is not the nature of regression; actually the rocking infants are retarded. They have been arrested in their development; they never had the opportunity to progress beyond the primary narcissistic investment. They were not offered the opportunity of forming the memory traces of an object, constant in time and space, and consistent with itself. They were not afforded the opportunity to invest the representation of privileged parts of their own bodies in action, counteraction, interaction, with the mother's body.(33)

In summary, inconsistent, contradictory behavior of the mother makes the establishment of adequate object relations impossible, and arrests the child at the level of primary narcissism, so that his libidinal drive is in the form of rocking.(34) It is only pathological when rocking becomes the main activity of the child and persists throughout the whole of the first year and later.(35)

'Some authorities hold that stuttering is the result of an organic brain disease or physiological defect, but that is still a moot question. The first hesitations and halts in a child's speech are as normal as the missteps, stumbles, and falls in the child's earliest attempts in walking, due to lack of coordination and control of the walking mechanism.'(36)

Stutterers, Dr. John Paul Brady notes, have the least trouble getting words out while they are singing or reading aloud in unison with others. And because rhythm seems to aid fluency, speech therapists have long used metronomes in retraining sessions with stutterers.(37)

Although there is no support for the hypotheses that rhythm exerts its control over the stutterer by causing the subject to focus his attention on some other activity, the results of an experiment by Fransella shows that speaking in time with a rhythmic beat elicits significantly fewer speech errors than does speaking in the absence of a rhythmic stimulus. It is possible that rhythmicity itself is related in some way to etiology of stuttering.

If there is an existing cardiac arrhythemia, there is an irregular heart action caused by disturbances, either physiological or pathological, in discharge of cardiac impulses from a node or their transmission through conductile tissue of the heart. A sinus arrhythmia is an irregular heart beat occurring commonly in children or in the aged in which the rate alternately increases and decreases.(39) In either case there is a characteristic impairment of rhythm which may interfere with one's life unless amelioration of this loss of rhythm is corrected. Rhythm and music, then, are often an unconscious but integral part of our lives.

'Almost all the music we know is, in one way or another, built on a duple concept. Why do we need this duplexity so badly? The answer is simple. Just think again of the human heart. Its pulse is not just 1, 1, 1, 1. In order to contract and pump its supply of blood into our arteries, the heart must first expand. Thus there are two phases to each heartbeat, expansion and contraction, 1-2, 1-2. That is the fundamental beat of all human life. Physical life is duple. We live in a world of up and down, back and forth, day and night."(41)

"That's why most music has duple meter, which means two beats per bar or some multiple of two beats per bar, like four, six, or eight."(42)

"Of course it's true that music is triple." One might even say that the three-concept is almost as fundamental as the two-concept. But note that I say almost; because three, basic as it is in music, is not grounded in our biological nature. It is not physical in its function. The heart just doesn't beat in ¾ time." "We are duple; perhaps that's part of our finiteness. If we could break through it we might begin to understand the universal problems that plague us. But the value of tripleness to music at least lies precisely in the contrast with dupleness. It is the first and noblest exception to our natural savage instinct of left-right. Three is an invented number; an intellectual number, it is primarily an unphysical concept. Perhaps that is why 3 has always been so mystical a symbol to man, as in the Holy Trinity.(43)

Van de Wall points out there is a common factor regarding music and the sensory motor reaction. The inhibiting function of the mentality, of which we are not always conscious, is not active. In the infant the mentality is not developed; in the mentally ill and deteriorated individuals it is impaired. If, then, all these persons react to musical stimuli with an involuntary sensory-motor action, that fact seems to indicate that the physiological motor response is the most basic, the earliest, and the most lasting reaction to music.(44)

Other sensory-motor reaction changes have been

studied. These studies have shown that music tends to cause changes in breathing, cardiac blood pressure, and blood supply. The tendency is more to increase the rate of these activities than to decrease it. Music which is strongly vigorous and rhythmic has a greater tendency to increase these physiological processes than other kinds of compositions.(45)

Chapter IV

Music Therapy Indications

In nearly all cultures music is one of the popular and appealing activities of social man because of its unique sensory appeal.

Because music provides basic, non-verbal communication, music therapy can be instrumental in the treatment of many mental disorders. Often a patient is unable to relate to a psychotherapist because of the sometimes threatening nature of a verbal relationship. Music therapy is designed to meet the needs of such patients through another, non-threatening therapeutic process.

While it is not feasible to list every type of human difficulty which might benefit from music therapy, the following examples of many problems where music therapy is applicable are listed to illustrate this discipline as a full, viable therapy for the mentally and physically ill.

Early Childhood Psychoses

All children, during the first year of life, appear to have the rudiments of ego function, which are developed through early sensory processes. Their thinking, therefore, is rudimentary. They demand immediate sensory gratification.(46) The first example, the autistic child, exhibits as characteristic symptoms an almost complete withdrawal and lack of interest in people, poor body identity, and a use of speech as sound making and as a private language, but not as communication with other people. Sometimes he is mute. Autistics are thought of as "treatment-resistant" because they lack responsiveness to the therapist. Rimland,(47) Kanner,(48) Bergman and Escalona(49) have written about the autistic child's preoccupation with, interest in, and memory for music. The rhythmic parts of music are deep lying factors in the physiological functioning of the autistic child. Rhythm can prevent mental development because of its regressive influence, but if the therapist uses these regressive elements as therapeutic tools in attempting to establish or re-establish human contacts, the same rhythm can aid development.

The autistic child rocks compulsively to a fixed metronomic beat, regardless of the rhythm at which music is played. Initially the therapist aligns himself to this beat by playing improvised music on the piano. Eventually he explores any kind of reaction to his improvisations which might be interpreted as the child's response to the music. When a response is observed, which may vary from a churlish grin to a fit of violent anger, he uses that particular stimulus which produced it, with new improvisational explorations. When he has enough material he carefully begins to change the musical beat, either faster or slower, in an attempt to raise or lower the rocking rate of the patient. If he can accomplish this, he then successfully interrupts the compulsive, non-discriminatory response pattern of the child. He has opened up an effective mode of communication, consequently creating the possibility for further therapeutic incursion.

Autistics usually replace word singing with humming or whistling. In an attempt to communicate with these children, first the key of their tune is determined, then the piano is used to accompany their song. Any reaction can become the initial foundation on which to build any future therapeutic relationship.

Another major childhood psychosis is symbioses. Compared with autistic children, symbiotic children are more highly developed,(50) and show a preference for singing instead of speech(51) as contrasted with the autistic's avoidance of words during his preoccupation with music. They exhibit a clinging relationship with their mother, who is making a desperate effort to keep her child dependent on her, even to the extent of overwhelming intrusion on the normal exploratory development of her child.

In addition to clinging behavior which continues past the early years, ritualistic behavior, panic or other severe anxiety reactions may be observed when separated from the mother. The child may show pronounced orality in the form of great pleasure derived from sucking, swallowing and biting. Schizophrenia, which is in simplest terms, a withdrawal from reality, can also occur in childhood, usually after the child is five or six years old. When the break from reality becomes maximal, the child derives his pleasures from the fantasies he creates in his withdrawal. He appears to be totally preoccupied with himself. He may exhibit unexplained fears of persecution and suspicions of other people.(52) Other symptoms include self-rejecting body image, extreme fears often of a sexual nature, and uncontrolled fantasies.

In such children a careful observer may discern an obsessive interest in music from phonograph records. Rocking, hallucinations, fantasies and over-excitement can become seemingly irresistable reactions to the musical stimulus. The pathology of these reactions, and the special use of music in treating the childhood schizophrenic are fully covered in the chapter entitled: *Fantasy Stimulated By Music.*

Underachievers

Mental retardation of subnormality are common clinical terms denoting limited intelligence. In recent years retarded children have been classified as being educable-retarded, trainable retarded or non-trainable. Special types of retardation include mongolism and cretinism. Retardation, of the degree of type, deprives the child of the opportunity of succeeding according to set rates of progress in regular classrooms, thus, many of them, are subject to failure in the course of their education, even if they are segregated to special classes. When such failure experiences become sufficiently common, obvious symptoms of withdrawal, frustration and anxiety result.

These emotionally unhealthy results in the underachieving child may not only impede his own adjustment and development, but also can threaten the mental health of his siblings. A good deal of attention has been paid to appropriate methods of supplying successful experiences to retarded children. If brought to treatment centers, efforts are made to make the child more efficient, proud of himself, responsibe to challenge, and healthier emotionally. This is done by capitalizing on whatever motor and intellectual abilities the patient may display. As a part of such endeavor, music therapy can be an important, sometimes decisive participant. The underachiever can develop interpersonal relationships through active musical experience, some of these for the first time. Consequently feelings of security, developing from a successful experience, could produce a marked improvement in his attitudes in the family. He may also disclose other learning assets, heretofore invisible, which could be subsequently used to advance his learning, and further support his ego.

Speech Defects

Because humans depend so largely on speech in order to communicate, problems in the forming of interpersonal relationship can sometimes lead to problems in the development of speech patterns. These difficulties often occur during the preschool years when the most rapid progress of speech development is taking place. Because communication is so largely dependent on speech, the development of speech is inextricably interwoven with the development of interpersonal relationships, thus, speech difficulties may arise from tensions in the interpersonal field. Other types of speech difficulties may result from organic factors such as malformation of the mouth, other physiological components of the speech aparatus, or neurological impairments.(53)

Speech difficulties are often expressed in stuttering. The stutterer experiences varying degrees of tension and anxiety, depending on the severity of his stuttering. Although he may seldom stutter when alone, or in the presence of children his own age, or with animals, any social situation where he perceives himself as pressured causes him to lose his rhythm; thus his previous dysfluency of speech recurs.(54)

The prognosis for the stutterer is poor if the difficulty extends into the second decade of his life. It is poorer still in the third, and beyond.(55) This is true even if intensive psychotherapy and conventional speech therapy is or has been applied.

Stutterers seem to have the least amount of difficulty with their stuttering when singing or reading aloud in unison with others. It has been known for some time that a basic problem with the stutterer is his disturbances in his speech rhythms. However, most available methods fail to show significant success in correcting this problem. Recently, a technique has been devised, in which an electronic metronome, placed inside a hearing aid, working concomitantly with suitably correlated behavior therapy, appears to relieve the anxiety that aggravates the speech problem.(56)

Because of the rhythmic elements and motivation it can produce, music can have a direct influence upon the stutterer. It has been found that a steady rhythm demands continuous attention and that speaking in time with a rhythmic beat can be effective in ameliorating chronic, severe stuttering in adults.(57)

Although research in the therapeutic applications of music to speech disorders is very scanty, we have some consistent evidence that stuttering, at least, will respond with improvement to certain specially designed speech and music therapy techniques.

A cleft palate is another cause of speech difficulty. This is a condition wherein there is a congenital fissure in the roof of the mouth, forming a link between the mouth and nasal cavities. Wind instruments have had the most significant amount of success with this disorder, because of their demand in exercising air control through the mouth rather than through the nasal passage. Articulation and communication difficulties are common. The primary purpose in the therapeutic use of wind instruments (kazoo, bamboo flutes, etc.) is to afford increased feelings of self-worth and achievement. Stimulating recreational activities are secondary goals, and can be recommended as additional resources in treatment after the person has developed some positive feelings about himself. This eliminates any premature failures, and increases the probabilities that meaningful musical experiences will occur.

Brain Dysfunction

The aphasic child is suffering from a massive, sometimes absolute, intrustion on his ability to communicate with speech. He is either unable to say what he wishes (expressive aphasia), or is unable to understand what is said or written (receptive aphasia). Both conditions are a consequence of brain damage, usually called brain dysfunction. When both expressive and receptive areas of the brain are involved, there is a total inability to communicate through speech.

Despite this he may elicit musical skills which require exploration in order to be of any therapeutic significance. Music helps improve the child's capacity to communicate in a non-threatening, often rewarding atmosphere.

There are a number of other types of brain dysfunctions where music therapy can be a valuable aid.

Hyperactivity, hypoactivity and disordered activity are three major categories of motor behavioral disorders. Both physical and emotional disturbances may be observed in all three problems. In hyperactivity, extreme restlessness and severe muscular tension are the principal observable symptoms. In hypoactivity, as a contrast, there is a drastic reduction in overall activity, subnormal muscle tone, or a complete loss of function of a muscle or a muscle group.

Apraxia (the inability to manipulate objects in a

purposive manner), or ataxia (the incoordination of the limbs or of any bodily function), exhibit disordered activity.(58) Such disorders, particularly when exhibited in a classroom, can frequently lead to underachievement or failure in the prescribed courses.

When the affected child has to meet daily limitations on his behavior, and is unable to discover suitable substitutes to satisfy environmental demands, he may suffer from strong feelings of incompetence and loss of self esteem.

The following is a description of methods which have been introduced into the application of music therapy and are designed to improve such conditions of motor incoordination.

The author has used the Free Arm Swing, described by Nordoff(59) with considerable efficiency. A sturdily mounted drum and cymbal are used, held at the right hand. Light weight tympani mallets are used. It is desirable to fit a knob to the inner side of the tympanis handles to give the patient a better grip. The drum and cymbal are then struck vigorously by the patient. The movement to strike begins above the head. The hands can beat together or alternately. This activity should be accompanied by stimulating music. Different registers of the piano can be used by the therapist to differentiate the strokes on the drum and cymbal. Robins(60) suggests the use of the tambourine as an instrument to assist in rhythmic coordination activities, and to help evoke reactions relating to communication. Although Robins has used this technique mainly with mentally handicapped children, the author finds it has worked well in developing rhythmic coordination in neurologically impaired children. In this procedure the patient is handed a tambourine and is instructed to follow the movements of a therapist who also has one. The therapist begins by placing the tambourine in his right hand and hitting with his left hand at a moderate rate of speed. He instructs the patient to do the same. The therapist can, at any time, increase or decrease the rate of speed, and or hit other parts of his body such as his elbow or foot. The same procedure then can be worked with the opposite hand.

Music therapy may be incorporated into efforts to improve problems of severely impaired body identity. This type of problem involves the patient's dissociation or loss of understanding of various body parts.

One of the techniques used to help strengthen identity and body awareness utilizes a body-sized wall mirror. As the patient stands in front of the mirror where his entire body is reflected, the therapist improvises songs which include the patient's name and/or parts of his body, thus making both visual and auditory experiences equally important. Another technique used to improve body identification might be called the "Do as I Do" method. This employs two tambourines, one for the patient, one for the therapist. The therapist holds a tambourine in one hand and hits it with the other. The patient watches. The therapist then directs the patient, "Do as I do." If this is successfully accomplished, then the therapist proceeds to include in the mimicry, the hand and/or elbow. This technique can be made more and more complex by combining various parts of the body in different patterns. Speed in this exercise is crucial. It should not exceed the speed comfortably attained by the patient. Judgment must be made as the therapist observes and evaluates the patient. If the therapist errs here, frustration and subsequent failure can ensue. The therapist must see to it that the patient has gained sufficient confidence, before the more complex patterns are introduced.

Incoordination or arrhythmia is exhibited in patients who are unable to repeat a simple rhythmic pattern even at a very slow speed. Because of the very nature of the deficits in these patients, they fail repeatedly in their attempts to do anything motorical. Such a patient must first be made aware of simple beats. The drum and cymbal are used. He beats with only one hand until he is comfortable and able to go ahead with a two beat pattern. The basic aim of introducing music therapy here is to make some kind of successful motorical performance a reality.

A further, rare area of music therapy application is in musicogenic epilepsy (reflex). This refers to a rare and hard to cure disease which is highlighted by epileptic convulsions precipitated by music. It appears that certain music can cause severe seizures in certain vulnerable individuals. In one particular patient, orchestrated music touched off fits. Dr. F. Forster et al. used 'extinction therapy' — a procedure which is designed to decrease the strength of the undesirable reaction. It was found that while extinguishing the stimulus which appeared to produce the seizures, other disturbing reactions to the music were also removed.(61)

In the realm of orthopedic difficulties music therapy has applications. The physically handicapped child must make use of any bodily skills and coordinations he has available in order to help him overcome threats to his social and emotional adjustment. The orthopedically disabled child's difficulty may range from any condition which reduces his physical activity significantly — such as a heart murmur or diabetes, to amputation or cerebral palsy. He may present a morbid or repulsive symptom to other people, either because of his gross physical handicap or its accompanying emotional disturbances. Clearly he may be strongly influenced by the ignorance and consequent rejection of the people in his social environment.

His maladjustment may reach an extreme when he is in school. Some of the attitudes held by supposedly responsible educators and parents include extreme pressures to overcome his resistance to separation from home and the imposition of standards of achievement beyond his capacity. The practice of threatening or bullying to conform to the schools conventional model of behavior, criticizing or nagging over his performance or social behavior, and parental overprotection that restricts the child's growing independence can be most damaging pressures. (62)

As with underachievers and neurologically impaired children, emphasis must be placed on the strengths of the orthopedically disabled child rather than deleteriously focusing on his weaknesses. In this sense music can not only be beneficial in helping develop new or better coordinated movements and corresponding muscle strength, but it also provides avenues wherein the patient can gain encouragement, increased self-esteem and ego gratification. In the last sense he makes gains through his new beliefs that he can be an accepted and productive human being.

To treat any patient properly it is essential that adequate clinical data is available. This should include medical, developmental, educational, psychiatric, psychological material and any available examinations pertaining to vision, hearing and laterality.

The most favorable environment for achievement is

one in which the strengths and weaknesses of the patient are fully and accurately assessed. Developmental level may vary considerably in such areas as eye-hand coordination, language, attention span, body identity, gross and fine motor coordination. It is necessary to determine these variations with a music therapy evaluation so that therapeutic possibilities relating to music therapy may be determined.

The primary function of this evaluation is to assess the rhythmic assets of the patient, that is, to determine the patient's ability in terms of sensitivity to 1. rhythmic patterns (simple to complex) 2. tempo (slow and fast) and 3. dynamics (loud and soft). Many patients who are referred to music therapy are usually those with a feeling of worthlessness and having deep feelings of being a failure as a human being so that discovery of assets in the evaluation is essential in giving a therapist vital data to set goals.

The secondary function of the evaluation is to discover the patient's deficits. If the patient is insensitive to the normal range of rhythmic patterns, this may indicate dysfunctions in the receptive and/or expressive or motoric developmental processes. The ability to perceive dynamics (from very soft to very loud) is then evaluated. When the patient has difficulty with the rhythmic range or tempo range, he usually has difficulty in the perception of dynamics.

PROCEDURE

The patient is given two drum sticks and instructed to use them on the drum and/or cymbal. The music therapist sits at the piano awaiting any sort of beat which he then repeats on the piano. In most cases the patients will begin to beat without hesitation, but in some cases the therapist will have to initiate the piano rhythms to stimulate the patient's beating. it is then without further verbalization between the therapist and patient that the therapist can assess the performance of rhythmic patterns, tempo, and dynamics.

After the patient gives the therapist rhythmic information on the drum and cymbal, that is, the rhythm and tempo that are most natural to the patient, the therapist can lead the patient from the simple patterns to the more complex ones conconmitant with tempo changes to determine

1 - which hand is preferred

2 - if incoordination exists with either hand or

3 - if the patient is functioning within normal rhythmic and tempo range.

At the same time the therapist can evaluate the sensitivity of the patient as to his perception in changes of dynamics. Menninger's statement that: the child attains satisfaction from hearing and seeing as well as from feeling, and music and art constitute the highest pinnacle which pleasurable hearing and seeing achieve(63) describes accurately the author's hopes for a successful union between psychiatry and music. Particular emphasis should be laid on the increased field of motivation afforded the hitherto unreachable patient by music therapy.

The verbal and non-verbal elements of music make special sensory training techniques possible. In the sensory field the primary categories which are available to the music therapist are auditory discrimination, audio-visual discrimination and skills, tactual discrimination and kinaesthetic perception. One major goal is the improvement of sensory skills and the broadening of the spectrum of sensory experiences. A diagnostically oriented music therapy evaluation can be effective support to the patient, and it should be considered as a fixed, reliable portion of the armamentarium of the professional therapeutic team for this purpose. Music therapy evaluation can be used to aid in assessing interests, special abilities, and evaluating the precise nature of pathological disturbances — particularly those whose clinical symptoms are primarily withdrawal, visual-motor and coordination difficulties and hallucinations.

Chapter V

Fantasies Stimulated By Music

Many of us, at one time or another, have heard a song and felt somewhat nostalgic. This is because music often stimulates an inner experience wherein memories and emotions, tied together by previous epxeriences, are re-aroused. The result is often a long string of reveries which probably would not have occurred if the person had not been listening to the music. Much of the material aroused has an imaginative or fantasy-like quality to it. Certainly, the experience is quite unlike the cold, rational reasoning involved in problem solving.

It is possible for fantasy to be either healthy or pathological. Probably the best way to determine whether the fantasy is healthy or not, is to examine the way in which the fantasy is put to use — is it constructive or destructive in the person's life? It may be the impetus for astoundingly creative discoveries or productions, as in the lives of scientists and artists, or it may stimulate or actually produce pathological elements in the person's thinking, such as psychotic delusions or hallucinations.

Music can bring associations locked in the mind to the surface. It can be the link between conscious and unconscious. In psychiatry the term association frequently refers to the relationship between the conscious and the unconscious, ideas in the former being connected to the latter. Associations may be free or induced. When the individual, without prompting, is encouraged to produce and expand upon an idea or ideas, the process is known as 'free' association.

Induced associations involve the presentation of

stimulus words. A word is given to the listener who then is requested to respond with the next word that comes into his head. Presumably the second word was in some way linked by a significant association to the first word.(64)

Altshuler states that pictorial associative music is played to stimulate imagery and associations. Through such music the calling up of various past associations is facilitated. Music leaves a 'memory' not only in the mind but in the emotional sphere, in the movements of the body and muscles. It is more easily recalled by the mental patient than anything else, for it is more firmly implanted in his system. Calling up past experiences means bringing into the mind of the mental patient basic realities.(65) Ainlay said it is difficult to imagine any patient in any hospital and especially an army hospital, who does not associate certain songs or music numbers with past experiences. And since all such experiences must be either pleasant or unpleasant, the tune will naturally tend to reproduce, at least temporarily, mental associations similar to the original experiences. It becomes at once apparent that great care should be exercised in the selection of music to be used, particularly in neuropsychiatric wards.(66)

Van de Wall also noted that activities instigated intellectually by music can have a pathological character.(67)

From its inception, psychoanalytic therory concerned itself with art, repeatedly comparing it to dream and myth, and to daydream and fantasy. It is Noy's opinion that Freud's negative attitude toward music has retarded much significant research in this area. Before 1920 psychoanalytic thinkers felt that music caused regression.(68) Most of the explanations at that time were derived through analysis of introspective experience or the analysis of others' similar experiences, not through experimental or clinical procedures.(69)

It is not the purpose of this book to explore the general regressive effects of music on a wide variety of personalities. The author will limit, therefore, his discussion to its effects on the psychotic child.

Since the discovery of the phonograph, authorities in the psychological and education fields noted that music presented to children through this medium facilitated educational progress and expanded the enjoyment of recreational activities.

The author has noted on a number of occasions, while observing indoor recreation classes with psychotic children, that a phonograph was played continuously throughout the period, apparently in the expectation that the music was having a generalized, beneficial effect on the group.

In one instance, there was only one staff member present to work with fifteen children. Obviously it was impossible for her to work closely with all of them simultaneously; thus, her individual attention was thinly and unevenly spread amongst the group members. Most of the children who were not being attended to rocked or withdrew from active responses to the environment. When they were given individual attention, this behavior ceased.

During a recess period the children and staff all gathered in the gym waiting for the next class to begin. Again music was played. The staff ignored it and many children were chatting among themselves. Some children, however, clearly responded to the music, often rocking actively to its rhythm. Others flapped their hands, twirled strings and gave considerable evidence of being preoccupied with the music. The author considered it greatly significant that though often displaying odd behavior during this time, these preoccupied children did not cause any trouble nor did they give any control problems to the staff. The author judged that the music, here regarded as a kind of innocuous addition to the environment, was really serving as a baby-sitting device, and was, indeed, not innocuous at all. It seemed to be producing uncontrolled fantasy reactions, some of them probably intensifying the very condition that the staff was trying to reduce or alleviate.

Further observations made by the author included three individual children, all of whom had emotional disturbances of psychotic types. Each clinically presented similar symptoms such as rocking, or indiscriminate laughter, hallucinations, or sexual fantasies of an uncontrolled nature which involved public and compulsive auto-eroticism.

Upon hearing music, all three children behaved as though they could no longer control their impulses. They seemed to be afraid of what they were experiencing. It seemed they treated the music as some overpowering stimulus about which they could do nothing. It made all of them afraid. Rocking in all three intensified. Facial contortions multiplied, indicating pain and increased anxiety. The children were apparently fantasizing in negative, more uncontrolled ways, and while doing so were unable to apply themselves to any sequential, environmentally directed activity. As soon as the music stopped, rocking immediately stopped too. Unpleasantness of mood, however, remained for an appreciable period afterward. Paradoxically, this seemingly unpleasant fantasy world into which the children withdrew, and the undesirable regressive behavior which accompanied it, appeared to be preferable to these children rather than their participation in realistic human relationships. Each one of the three children reacted strongly to the content and dynamics of the music. Although the music varied in form and style, the childrens' reactions were specifically related to the volume, harmonic quality (consonant or dissonant) sudden changes in frequency, instrumental timbre, mood of the music and tempo. In each case, when the music was played without the interaction or intrusion of the therapist, the above mentioned elements seemed to elicit psychotic withdrawal as evidenced by the quality of the fantasy. The children seemed to use the music as a stimulus to further remove themselves from the real world. They appeared to use each element of the sound as a guide to reacting against frightening forces within themselves.

Music represents a defense against the paranoid situation. At the same time music affords a defense against the melancholic situation as a means of guilt denial and preservation of the loved object. Music is a defensive instrument in the form of identification with the aggressor, which gives the power to overcome the bad objects. Music, representing also the good object, conveys the feeling of conquest of the superego, and because of the music structure, also of surrender to the superego.(70)

The regressive and fantasy-producing effects of music have been reported by many investigators (Bardas, 1919; Teller, 1917; Alvin, 1965; Germain, 1928; Van den Daele, 1967).(71) However, there are no careful studies of the use of music in treating the psychotic.

The author has done a number of studies which

indicate, that though the indiscriminate application of music to the psychotic child is harmful, and often destructive, a carefully controlled application can be most useful. Special techniques have to be devised to make such applications effective. These studies indicate that music can be used to increase the attention of psychotic children to the environment, and attach them more closely to constructive, reality-oriented activities. The principle used is based on the concept that music can be used as a reward and in this way help to modify behavior along modern conditioning techniques.

The cases in the following chapter were discussed in order to demonstrate how this principal, as well as the other concepts in music therapy can be applied.

Chapter VI

Mark, Joe and Robert

Background Information

Mark, the second of three siblings, was white, and seven years, five months old when he was enrolled at the hospital.

His father was a lieutenant in the local fire department, who moonlighted in his off hours as a paper hanger. His wife described him as a very active, affectionate husband, who was warm and supportive both to his wife and children. She felt he was the stronger, more enthusiastic parent.

Mark's mother was a very pretty woman, of normal intelligence, who seemed capable of emotional expression and warmth. She apparently found it difficult to accept the existence of any serious difficulty in Mark, and believed his main problem was speech retardation. She had strong hopes he would develop into an average, normally bright boy.

Both parents described Mark as being readily accepted by his siblings, though, curiously, he did not play with them. Rather, he played alone, not including himself in their activities nor them in his. Sometimes he displayed sudden severe temper outbursts during which he occasionally attacked his younger sister, though never doing her any serious physical harm.

According to his mother, he was a full-term baby, delivered normally. He weighed eight pounds, twelve ounces at birth with no deformities or peculiarities noted during his stay at the hospital. He was bottle fed — and his demand was regulated by the mother according to a strictly kept schedule. He began feeding himself at one year. Toilet training commenced at two years and was fully accomplished three months later. No unusual incidents or difficulties appeared during this training. Mark's motor development seemed normal. He walked at one year and his coordination and gait appeared normal. At two years, however, his vocabularly still consisted only of "mama' and "dada." His speech development was slow enough for the mother to seek medical consultation. Upon doing this, she obtained a diagnosis of 'organic encephalopathy' with mental retardation. His only recognized illness during this period was chicken pox.

Both parents reported that Mark had always been a good child, 'too good,' as the mother expressed it. They had done a good deal of reflecting on his past, and the mother noted that while her pregnancy was normal, she now thought that Mark never behaved like the other two children after he was born. He would lie in his crib after awakening, apparently fully alert and content, but never crying for a bottle.

Quite early in his infancy Mark showed he disliked being held or rocked during his feeding times. He preferred to consume the bottle lying propped in the crib. At about two and a half, Mark showed little anxiety, or actually any type of emotional response when the parents left the house, nor did he greet them with visible recognition signs when they returned.

At about four to five years old Mark showed his capacity to learn selected things. After watching T.V. programs he began to mimic some of them. He can now name the programs. He knows the order of their appearance during the day. He clearly becomes interested in some of them.

Mark was enrolled in nursery school at four and a half years, awaiting placement at a residential school for the retarded. While in nursery school, his speech improved somewhat, however, he was never seen to speak directly to another person unless he wanted to satisfy an immediate need. Although his attention span at the nursery school was limited to only a few minutes directed at one task or object, he did take his own initiative to play, sing and listen to records. Mark is extremely careful to avoid injury to his body. He is physically active, but always chooses activities which keep him from getting cut or bruised.

At six years a psychological evaluation was done, but Mark would not cooperate unless his mother was present. He whined and fretted continually, and showed no interest or enthusiasm for the tests. Sporadically he would say 'cry' or 'don't cry.' His mother explained that he usually copied these expressions from her when he was threatening to cry.

In the testing process Mark made several drawings resembling faces. He held the crayon easily and evidenced no difficulty in manipulating it. He did not perform on the Seguin Form Board unless his mother urged him to do so, however, he finally did complete this test at the sixty to sixty-five month level, a score about one year below his chronological age.

From test results and clinical observations the examiner summarized his findings by noting that Mark was severely emotionally disturbed. He was judged as angry at his mother, while at the same time more than normally dependent on her.

The diagnostic impression given to the parents, when Mark was six, and at the residential treatment center was chronic brain syndrome of unknown cause with secondary perceptual and expressive disorder, and with superimposed emotional reaction. This condition was supposed to have some resemblance to autism, the opinion probably based on relatively isolated communication behavior.

Music Therapy Evaluation

Reason For Referral

Mark was referred for a music therapy evaluation by the examining psychiatrist, after other efforts to test or evaluate him proved fruitless. It was felt that Mark's singing and intensive listening to records were positive reactions to music and a possible lead to communication with him.

Exploratory Observations

Mark was physically well developed, personable and attractive in appearance. The boy smiled slightly upon entering the therapist's office as the therapist greeted him with outstretched hand. Mark voluntarily approached and shook hands, and said 'hello.'

He sat down and remained quiet as the therapist sat down. His attitude seemed to be that of polite waiting for further instructions. Little anxiety was noted.

He picked up a tambourine, examined it closely and shook it appropriately. The therapist began to shake one too. Mark started to follow and imitate the therapist's movements and rhythms.

A few minutes later the therapist introduced tone bells. Mark took them and played them with apparent pleasure, continuing to follow the therapist. The therapist sang "Hello Mark." Mark, with no apparent difficulty, was able to follow, singing the words and reaching correct pitch.

In conversation Mark showed echolalic type repetitiveness to sentences and did not appear to understand their real meaning. His articulation was poor and voice quality was low and nasal.

Further difficulties arose when the Rhythmic Associative Test was introduced. Mark could only distinguish and play two of the four different rhythmic patterns. Each pattern, exhibited on a different instrument, was supposed to represent the particular instrument on which it was played. After five minutes Mark showed clear frustration. He tried and succeeded on two instruments to copy the patterns, and failed on a third. He lost interest, began to verbally perseverate, and went to the closest door and opened it. This appeared to be his way of changing tasks. In general, however, Mark's cooperation was judged as good. He seemed eager to do his best. From time to time he glanced at the therapist for signs of approval and was visibly pleased when they were forthcoming.

Summary

Mark seemed in contact with and well oriented to his immediate surroundings. He rocked back and forth on his feet at one point in seeming indecision rather than withdrawal. He made no attempts at physical contact with the therapist, but did make obvious gestural and verbal attempts to communicate.

Since it had been reported that Mark had neurological deficits, probably of an aphasic nature, both receptive and expressive, it appeared that the language problem was basic. It probably caused both the social and emotional isolation Mark was reported to have shown from infancy. It was this isolation which lead to the psychiatric impression of autism.

Mark's musical abilities were judged to be both meaningful and constructive. He exhibited genuine satisfaction in his actions with the instruments.

He did show evidence of a compulsive beat in his reactions to the instruments. This type of beat may be defined as a fixed tempo which appears as soon as a child is able to copy rhythmic models. No matter what model is offered for mimicry, the child responds with this same tempo. It is as unvarying as a metronome fixed at one speed.

A child who beats compulsively seems unable to voluntarily respond in any other way to a tempo which lies outside his compulsive best. He may show varying responses to the harmonic, melodic, or even rhythmic structure of the music, but behaviorally he seems unable to match the tempo of the given music with a simliar one of his own.

The therapist felt that repeated presentation of different, but extremely simple rhythmic patterns might possibly intrude on this compulsive beat pattern, and help Mark to alter it voluntarily.

It should also be noted that though he held drum sticks in both hands, Mark would only use his right hand to beat. He would put the right hand beater down and transfer the left hand beater to the right hand.

Recommendations:

1 — Referral was made to the speech department for a closer evaluation of his language difficulties.

2 — Musical activities were to be encouraged, but with emphatic precaution not to use pressure of any kind in the procedure.

3 — Music therapy was indicated for the purpose of

supporting and encouraging whatever visible assets in communication and person-to-person responsiveness existed in Mark. It was also indicated to correct his rhythmic dysfunction.

Music Therapy

Mark's initial session was uneventful. He waited outside the therapist's office for at least fifteen minutes without making any attempt to announce his arrival. Only when the therapist opened the door to look for him did he timidly indicate his presence and hesitatingly enter the office.

As soon as the door was closed Mark began to explore all the office areas in a methodical manner. He trifled with the piano keys while he flipped over the pages of a book. He then went quickly to the therapist's desk and repeatedly pushed the switch on the desk lamp on and off. Then his attention fixed on the desk calendar. He began to mutter in a low, almost unintelligible voice, "What month is it?" He turned each calendar page until he reached the end, then began again.

When asked if he would like to play the tone bells, Mark echoed, "Tone bells?" and excitedly ran over to the closet. With one of the bells in his hand, he quickly touched or looked at other pieces of equipment in the closet but showed no special interest in any of its contents.

When the therapist again directed his attention to the tone bells, Mark spontaneously played and sang "Hello" as he did in the music therapy evaluation. Then, as the therapist played the "Hello" on the piano, Mark sang in tune. While holding himself rigid, he beat in time in short, irregular bursts. At this point, quiet unexpectedly, he drew very close to the therapist partially sitting on the therapist's lap, but somehow remained defensive and untrusting. Clearly he was exploring our ability to relate.

As soon as the therapist stopped playing, Mark stood up and began to rock. When his attention was redirected to the tone bells, he stopped rocking and resumed playing.

The following sessions focused on strengthening the verbal areas by attempting to have him sing more and in more words as he played along with the therapist. The therapist further attempted to change and expand his compulsive beating by trying to make him more consciously aware of himself and his surroundings.

Each session consisted of a good morning song using Mark's name and a brief tone bell activity. The therapist then introduced a specially composed song dealing with names and physical situation of the body parts. Different instruments were also introduced. At first it was difficult to focus Mark's attention on his body parts. When the therapist began to use a large mirror, Mark's attention became more consistently fixed on the task at hand and he attempted to say the words for body parts by silently mouthing them while watching the therapist's lips in the mirror. No significant improvement in the intelligibility of his speech was noted however.

Since Mark would or could not use the two drumsticks simultaneously and appeared confused if this method were suggested to him, the therapist suggested using one drumstick. This improvisation seemed to put him more at ease.

In an attempt to produce a greater number of visible responses from Mark, and in particular to change his compulsive beat, improvisations were also made with a simple repetitive rhythmic pattern, played on the piano. The beat, however, was identical to the beat he produced in the music therapy evaluation, and continued at the same rate.

The therapist made a number of attempts to discover if Mark could perceive changes in tempo. The speed of the piano playing was increased and decreased in various orders, but Mark did not indicate he perceived these changes by any consistent response. His beat remained steady, with no dynamic change, even when the therapist added verbal instructions to the changes in playing. Whenever the therapist stopped playing and took time out for a rest, Mark would use the interval to go over to the closet to investigate every article in it, with the same minuteness and method he previously displayed. At times he would hold an article in his hand, and name it in a questioning-like tone. He seemed dissatisfied with the therapist's acknowledgement of his naming these articles, but continued to name them with what appeared to be increased anxiety as manifested by intensified verbality and body action. When the therapist asked if he would like to resume playing, he would usually back off from the closet, muttering, avoiding eye contact and rocking.

After twelve sessions Mark was able to play a specially composed drum and cymbal song, using two sticks simultaneously, one for the drum, the other for the cymbal. This was a significant advance in coordinated movement.

Mark's rhythmic confusion had been eliminated through the use of two different repetitive rhythmic patterns. There was some success in breaking down his complusive beating pattern. With the change in the beat pattern he began to beat much louder, and though he was following interjected tempo changes within his rhythmic range, he did not respond to any of the dynamic changes the therapist introduced in the playing. Mark's rhythmic pattern was a simple triplet. For example the pattern would parallel the three syllables in the word 'merrily.'

Spontaneous verbalization increased with the presumed decrease in anxiety. At the beginning of one session he asked, "Where's the stick?" When the therapist replied, "In the closet. I'll open it with my key," he said, "I'll do it."

In the following session the therapist was sitting in a chair next to the desk. Mark looked at the therapist, and, after fiddling with the objects in the closet and the drum and cymbal, said, "Come here." For the first time in all of the sessions Mark then smiled, certainly a hopeful change in a child whose affective life had, to this point, appeared so constricted.

Conclusion

In order to free Mark from his compulsive beat, the therapist had to make contact with Mark's rhythmic responses. From this the therapist had to proceed with helping the boy alter his compulsive pattern and lead him to some awareness of the existence of many other beat patterns.

Once Mark's compulsive beat was expanded, and therefore the apparent compulsive response broken, the boy exhibited increased appropriate verbalization and, for the first time, positive emotional responses. It is possible to consider that he became aware of tempo change. Certainly the new responses were significantly more healthy than his previous behavior had been.

JOE

Background Information

Joe, age sixteen, was born of an uncomplicated but unwanted pregnancy. His older brother was so aggressive, so difficult to train and control and so destructive in the household that the mother apparently decided she neither wanted nor could handle another child. As a possible result of being unable to face the reality of being pregnant with Joe, the mother developed a severe postpartum depression.

The older brother, who was four at Joe's birth, reacted with strong fears and aggressive jealousy to Joe's arrival. Reportedly he tried to push Joe's head through a windowpane and on other occasions expressed the desire to flush Joe down the toilet.

In addition the mother reported constant parental conflict. She complained of her husband's alcoholism. She noted her older son went into an institution for (undescribed) mental disturbances. She stated that the quarrels between herself and her spouse resulted in the father's disappearance from the house. He would stay away anywhere from a few days to a few weeks. This occurred throughout the marriage. A separation eventuated when Joe was sixteen.

In appearance the mother was frail. In demeanor she was extremely anxious and infantile. She came from a quite wealthy family and apparently had all her whims unquestioningly satisfied during her childhood and adolescence, resulting in very little capacity to deal independently with frustration or ability to control her impulses.

She had ulcers for eighteen years — dating from the time of the birth of Joe's older brother. She underwent an operation for them when Joe was twelve.

Her attitude toward Joe was ambivalent. She showed some affection, alternating with marked dislike and rejection. Her capacity to display genuine affection toward him was limited. She seemed continually fearful that Joe's behavior would be as aggressive and difficult to control as was his brother's. She wanted this boy to be placid, quiet and malleable. The interviewer decided that Joe, in order to gain any measure of visible approval or affection from his mother, had to become almost completely passive, play female type domestic roles and copy his mother's negative, distrustful attitude toward males.

Joe was reported to be a full term baby, born without visible physical abnormality. He weighed six pounds. He was bottle fed for one year. He was toilet trained at thirteen months without untoward incident. He was described as a 'good' baby who required little special attention because he could remain quiet for long periods of time, and was rarely crying or cranky. As a toddler he was quiet. He liked playing by himself. He was not active in his play. He showed little of the curious exploratory activity often characteristic of this age. His mother remembered none of his other developmental milestones accurately — such as teething or walking age. The only childhood illness she could remember was measles, at six years.

In school, from first grade on, Joe complained of stomach aches, and was often kept out of school. In the sixth grade he was apparently bullied by a group of older boys who teased him by calling him "baby." A boy once punched him in the stomach during the lunch period. Joe began to associate eating with bullying. At about the same time, a neighbor told him he could choke to death on bones in food. Joe thereupon began to avoid any food he thought had bones in it. He then read, in a first aid book, that people died after swallowing pins. From then on his feelings about food crystallized into a generalized food phobia. He no longer just worried about bones in food. He became frightened about eating in school, and stopped taking his lunch there. Shortly thereafter, at twelve, he became a school drop-out. He apparently was wholly unable to concentrate on school life because of his emotional difficulties, yet his only activities at home were to go out aimlessly into the yard, or go shopping with his mother. By the time he was fourteen he had advanced his phobia to the point where he refused to go out of the house.

Joe was taken to a state hospital for evaluation. While there, he refused to eat for two weeks and was force-fed. The dianostic impression given was psychoneurotic disorder, gastrointestinal reaction. The psychiatrist in charge noted "the food phobia appeared to be secondary to internalized aggression from the environment, and was not derived from a paranoid psychotic basis. In addition, feminine identifications had become habitual." Two years later it was recommended that he be sent to a residential treatment center to get away from his pathological family environment at which time the parents were given a diagnosis of anxiety reaction with schizoid features and psychosomatic complaints. Although testing showed he had average intelligence, he was unable to fully use it because of disjointed thought processes caused by abrupt mood while on the other hand he resorted to abusive name calling or a total submissiveness which could be associated with the overwhelming guilt about his destructive feelings towards his parents.

He was further described as emotionally immature,

with a poor self-concept and an obvious capacity for regression. His capacity for reality testing was marginal. He showed an almost complete passive-receptive attitude towards others in his social environment. His dependency needs seemed largely unfulfilled. He was greatly conflicted in his desire to show aggression. His social judgment was very poor. Tendencies towards anti-social behavior were noted.

On the W.A.I.S. he achieved a verbal score of 95, performance score of 87 and full scale score of 91. On the achievement tests his highest score was in vocabulary. Language, grammar and word usage were very low. Apparently he had never been able to discipline himself toward sustained study.

Music Therapy Evaluation

Reason For Referral

Joe was referred by his psychotherapist for a music therapy evaluation because he showed an interest in playing the drums, and responded to admiration when he played them in his unit. The purpose of the evaluation was to determine any special musical abilities he possessed and any supporting interests in this field.

Exploratory Observations

Joe was first seen at his home unit by the therapist as part of a group therapy interview. Simultaneously attending were four of his peers, all of whom had varying musical interests. Joe, when contrasted with his rather verbal and extroverted peers, acted shy and introverted. His sloppy dress and grooming, somehow redeemed his managing to look arty.

Joe displayed a sensitivity to rhythm and its components such as patterns and cadences. He also stated almost incessantly his intense desire to become a drummer.

He reacted to praise from either his peers or the therapist with every indication of irritated frustration. At times he also added statements of feelings of worthlessness, rejection and helplessness. He was, at the same time, critical and often loudly abusive toward the less capable members of the group.

A second evaluation was held one week later on an individual basis to explore further possible treatment for him.

On this occasion Joe entered the therapist's office happy over the fact that he had been 'picked' out of the group to receive private lessons, although he was confused as to why he alone was chosen. The therapist explained that he had not been chosen for music lessons, but further investigation about his musical interests. Joe seemed to accept this explanation and proceeded uncomplainingly with the evaluation.

He exhibited a high degree of ability to concentrate and respond sensitively to tempo changes, alterations in dynamics and changes in rhythm.

Despite his apparent success which the therapist applauded, a look of despair came over Joe. He expressed feelings of worthlessness, rejection and helplessness. He stated that his efforts were always for naught in yielding him satisfactions. He believed he was and always had been unable to reach the high expectations set for him by others of emotional importance in his life. Certainly, then, he had been unable to obtain any ego satisfaction in terms of believable achievement.

Summary:

Joe was the product of a pathological family atmosphere containing an overprotective mother and an alcoholic father who related unsuccessfully to his wife. Joe grew up without a reliable male model. His fear of not being able to become an adequate male was reinforced by his mother's desire to keep him passive, and her attempts to keep him in seclusion and away from rough children's play.

Joe's symptoms became aggravated in adolescence. He adopted a lethargic attitude toward every day events. He was persistently submissive to any display of authority. He would habitually express aggressive ideas, but didn't seem to feel the parallel emotions which would normally accompany them. His actions did not display the emotions he expressed.

His extreme introversion was exemplified in the school setting where, though he functioned well academically, he demanded 'bottle fed' encouragement by persistently degrading himself before the teacher authority. He habitually indulged in anti-social behavior outside of school, but blamed his actions on others. Marked swings of mood were observed, from defiant teasing to complete submissiveness.

Joe initially reacted to the therapist's request to play the drums by expressing feelings of inadequacy and worthlessness; however, such remarks seemed designed to elicit support and encouragement. This, Joe felt, diminished the weight of the demands for performance placed upon him.

Recommendations:

1 — All musical activities which, for Joe were socially acceptable were to be encouraged.

2 — Music lessons on the drums were recommended for the purpose of providing him with a meaningful outlet for creative self-expression, thus he might gain confidence in himself and a more positive life outlook.
3 — Music therapy on an individual basis was indicated, particularly in the light of Joe's very low self-esteem. Such therapy had as its goal the relief of the extreme peer pressure he felt, and possibly provide a way for him to construct healthy relationships with his peers.

Music Therapy

Joe entered the office and greeted the therapist in a mild, timid manner. He focused his attention immediately on the drum set. He asked the therapist if they could play together as they had done before, then, abruptly, he apologized in a piteous tone of voice for his lack of ability and talent in music.

The therapist noted he had a sullen and despairing look, and asked Joe if he would like to talk about the feelings he seemed to be having. Joe replied, "Ah, what's the use, let's play."

After playing several songs together with the therapist which sounded quite good, Joe dropped the drumsticks and said, "See, I stink." The therapist asked, "Why do you think so?"

Joe began a narrative, telling the therapist how 'everyone' thought he was a great musician. He commented on how laughable that was, how people were easily fooled. Everyone was fooled but his uncle. He said that his uncle had always ridiculed his interest in drums, telling him that drums were stupid instruments because a melody could not be played on them.

From the psychiatric summary comes this quote: "This sympathy-provoking device was seen by the psychiatrist in charge of the team as a defense against reality. It was designed to avoid the intrusion of real life facts on his fantasy thinking. Further, he would set up this frustrating situation to serve his punitive superego. When it was satisfied, he would swing into a transitional state of positive compliance. This temporary state was used to undo his negative self-image of the first stage. This was judged to be a healthy attempt to avoid identity diffusion at a regressed level, since the psychosexual problem of puberty is to achieve identity.

As soon as his negative image was undone through compliance, he retreated into his first stage with some pathological embellishments. He not only reverted back to the sympathy-provoking theme, but would leave each session trying to convince the therapist that his family was to blame for all of his difficultics and was solely responsible for his lack of self-respect and confidence."

The therapist felt that Joe's ego function, i.e., identity, relationships to reality, etc., were impaired and in need of supportive relationship therapy. The therapist decided to try and capitalize on his assets (rhythmic acuity) on a one to one basis, rather than try to build up his deficits at this time.

The most meaningful and rewarding experiences in any of the sessions that followed were those that included the use of a tape recorder. Joe and the therapist recorded themselves on tape, Joe playing the drums and the therapist playing the piano. During these recording sessions, Joe looked relaxed, and unusually interested in what he was doing. Upon hearing the duo on the recorder, Joe blushed with embarassment on several occasions while furtively glancing at the ceiling. Such tape recording sessions seemed to lessen his manifested anxiety.

Joe initiated buying a used drum set in order to play in a rock and roll band in his unit. When one of the members of the group ridiculed his drum set, Joe broke them up and set them on fire. They were totally destroyed.

This harmful incident was followed by a Christmas vacation at home which apparently proved traumatic, probably because the family situation was no better and its effects struck him just as badly as they did before he left home. When he returned, paranoid ideation and frequent periods of depression were observed. Joe refused to come to his music therapy sessions for two months despite many attempts by the therapist to get him to do so. The boy kept claiming he wanted to 'make it' with his peers in his unit, none of whom were musical. This is a good example of his unrealistic goal construction.

His attitude toward the therapist became more untrusting even hostile when the therapist tried to help him with his confusion.

After two months, during which time the therapist kept the boy's appointments open, and while he appeared periodically at the unit for meetings with the therapist, Joe requested a continuation of the sessions. The boy made a strong point of apologizing for his 'childlike behavior.'

The opportunity arose during the summer for Joe to have individual drum lessons with a music therapy trainee. The following is quoted from the trainee's personal observations:

"Joe's facility of comprehension as well as his improvisational proficiency soon gave definite indication of rhythmical capability; yet Joe expresses negative reactions to learning anything new, saying such things as "I can't do it." He realizes that as his knowledge of technique increases his proficiency will improve; yet he says he does not wish to learn more than rudimentary material because he feels safe in applying this present level of achievement.

As instruction continued, Joe's negativism decreased significantly. A reverse teaching technique had been effective in minimizing this negative behavior as well as increasing his attentiveness. I play an exercise, telling him that I shall purposely make a mistake. He is then instructed to give me its location and play it correctly by himself."

After the trainee left, Joe said that the trainee had tried to belittle and degrade him. He appeared to be jealous of the trainee's drum ability. Joe told many persons that he had learned nothing from the drum teacher, but had picked up his newly-acquired skill by himself. He did admit to the therapist on one occasion only, that he learned a lot from the summer sessions.

His musical motivation began to decline as there became apparent such pathological emotions as hate, destructiveness, jealousy, envy and paranoid delusions. This behavior seemed to be aggravated by his knowledge of the therapist's approaching marriage. Joe projected his disturbances onto the therapist in the form of obscene letters and constant verbal denunciations.

Rapid changes in the visible personality indicated conflicting motivations. He behaved in self-defeating ways on one hand, and asked for help on the other. He was demanding and compliant in turn. He gave evidence of ability to think clearly and profitably, and then hid this in a sudden fear that he would be shown up for his deficiencies.

The therapist decided to interrupt the treatment because it was felt that an interval of no therapy might give Joe a chance to calm down, and perhaps change his self-destructive actions, through insight. It seemed apparent that Joe was becoming too dependent and attached to the therapist, and the interruption might also help reduce this.

During the two month interruption of therapy, Joe first attempted to insult and humiliate the therapist by clumsy, angry, phone calls and similar letters. He then wrote a highly emotional apology which the therapist interpreted as an attempt on Joe's part to reinstate himself into good grace. The fear of losing the therapist was vividly apparent. The therapist answered by resuming music therapy.

It should be noted that Joe's therapy had not been totally abandoned during this interruption. Another therapist- an analyst- had been assigned to him in the interim.

Conclusion:

Although Joe's symptomatic behavior continued, he appeared to have gained new, healthy insight and emotional strength. This was exemplified by his initiation of musical activity at this unit. He ultimately progressed to a point where he was able to publicly perform at a high level of musicality-playing with professional musicians. He continued his drum lessons-emphasizing improvement of technique and application.

ROBERT

Background Information

Robert, a white, thirteen year old child was the second oldest of four children. When he was seven, he was diagnosed by a private psychiatrist as a schizophrenic reaction of the childhood type.

Robert was a full-term, normally delivered baby. He was bottle fed for two years. Toilet training was begun at one year and not completed until he was three and a half.

He developed a fear of toilets from unknown causes. It was so severe, that on a number of occasions he had to be taken to a physician because he held his feces so long. He was also eneuretic, but this ceased when he was between five and six. He was a head banger and a rocker from about eight months. Head banging ceased when he was one year. Rocking did not. Until he was two, Robert rocked constantly in his crib. His first recognizable word was 'light.' Then he said nothing more that was intelligible for two years. His speech later improved so that at about six and a half years he was able to carry on normal conversations, though he occasionally intermixed some nonsense words.

Robert always attended private schools, beginning with nursery school. His behavior in all schools was similar. He did not play or noticeably interact with other children, but withdrew instead. Upon the advice of a teacher, robert wa's taken to a private psychiatrist where he received the schizophrenic diagnosis.

When tested five years later he showed a full scale WISC of 80, primitive, expansive Bender drawings and projective test protocols (Rorschach and Blacky) giving evidence of a psychotic disorder based on very unhealthy relationships with his mother. He showed arrest and regression in psychosexual development. There was considerable difficulty in instinctual control.

At one private school for emotionally disturbed children when he was between eight and ten, he seemed to learn more behavioral control and made better contact with his environment. He would sit in his chair for longer periods, and more frequently carry out instructions. His learning capacity increased though he continued to indicate difficulty in abstracting and conceptualizing.

Just before he left this school he displayed 'autistic hand flapping, hopping and blinking.' Also he had been noted to 'smell books and papers and sometimes put them to his lips.'

In the next couple of years, while attending prep school, Robert became a behavior problem. He showed such poor impulse control and so much rocking that he disturbed classes. He frequently became abusive, and his mother was forced to remain in the building to take over in situations in which he became uncontrollable.

This behavior forced his withdrawal from the school. He commenced attending special classes in a local psychiatric hospital where he received intensive psychotherapy. Eventually it was recommended that he be placed in a residential treatment center.

There is a history of mental illness in the family. Robert's older brother, sixteen, was diagnosed as schizophrenic when he was ten. He is now attending High School, somewhat improved, but still showing odd behavior patterns.

The father, a fifty year old graduate of an Ivy League college, is a partner in a lucrative family business. He seems to be a suspicious, taciturn man, reportedly very sparing with his time and attention toward his children. He was reluctant to talk about his older son. The younger sisters, seven and eight, have presented no unusual problems.

The mother, an attractive woman of forty, easily broke into tears or displays of anger as she discussed her sons. Although she had been describing Robert's unusual and abnormal behavior to various interviewers (social workers and doctors) for years, she was barely able to acknowledge he had serious emotional problems until he was twelve. Even now she is unrealistic about his illness, and talks of his 'outgrowing' it soon.

She informed Robert he was going to a new 'school.' It was under this impression that he was admitted to this treatment center. His behavior at this time included running around nude in his apartment, frequent masturbation in the presence of his siblings, eneuresis and paranoid ideation. In addition, he was markedly depressed, obsessed about cars, and seemingly hallucinated on occasion.

Music Therapy Evaluation

Reason For Referral

Robert was referrred for a music therapy evaluation by his unit psychiatrist because of his compulsive interest in music. He would sit and listen intently, his attention accompanied by facial contortions and constant rocking.

Exploratory Observations

Robert looked average in development, gait and size, though his musculature appeared soft and underdeveloped.

Upon entering the office, he immediately began to talk about the model, year, and make of various automobiles. He then turned to repeat requests to be returned to the former hospital where he was a patient and where he could be properly nursed.

During the session a whole gamut of abnormal behavior took place including rocking, hysterical laughter, urinating in his trousers, exhibitionistic masturbation and constant repetitious conversation relating to food. He perseverated a great deal about things totally unrelated to the immediate situation. It appeared as though he were trying to keep the therapist at a safe distance, emotionally speaking. On other occasions during the session, Robert expressed fantasies involving retreat into the past where he though of himself as happier, because he was free to do entirely what he wanted to do.

He also discussed phonograph records intensively. He related certain specific records to particular past dates in his life, each characterized as a 'good' or a 'bad' year. If the therapist attempted to amplify these discussions, seeking Robert's ways of identifying good and bad, the boy only responded with words he had made up and had no meaning.

When music was introduced, Robert displayed a fine ability to follow difficult rhythmic patterns and was sensitive to dynamic and tempo changes. These abilities were evaluated through the use of instruments chosen because of their simple nature. Beating instruments, such as drums were most useful for this purpose.

The therapist first instructed Robert to repeat a simple rhythmic pattern on the drum. It was a pattern which the therapist first improvised on the piano. Then the therapist played a different rhythmic pattern on the piano and instructed Robert to repeat it on the cymbal. The therapist then added two more drums. Robert was able to distinguish and play four dissimilar rhythmic patterns, each on a different instrument.

The therapist proceeded to show Robert a selection of records. Upon recognizing one of his favorites, he immediately asked the therapist to play it on the record player. As soon as he heard the first strains of music from the record, he began to run around the room throwing his arms in the air, groaning in a low, buzzing sounds. Suddenly he sat down and started to rock furiously, apparently in some accord with the perceived changes in the music. When the therapist turned off the music Robert became anxious and sad and continued to rock. At this point in the session Robert refused to engage in any further discussion or activity.

Summary:

Robert's behavior appeared to be a stream of disjointed and unrelated activities. He habitually retreated from the therapist's attempts to form a good relationship by using unpleasant mannerisms, many of them apparently calculated to be annoying. There was just one point in the session where some continuity between the therapist's efforts and Robert's responses appeared. During the presentation of improvised rhythmic patterns he showed himself able to follow sudden changes in dynamics, tempo and rhythms with a marked degree of sensitivity and concentration.

Two things were apparent; Robert's defense system involved warding off intrusion into his private world with a highly elaborated set of behavioral patterns; second, that his world could be penetrated using certain rhythms, and interest could be sustained at least for brief time periods.

It was the therapist's interpretation of the emotional

dynamics displayed in the session that Robert's inadequate feelings, associated with his basic limitations and emotional vulnerability, left him unable to cope with or to develop normal social concepts. His desire to be nurtured was overwhelming in its force, and infantile in its expression. He worried continually about his inadequacy in social situations, and pyramided his anxieties by constant self-blaming. In spite of the difficulties of communication, however, the therapist judged Robert as genuinely able to express his feelings in ways that could be consistently understood and responded to therapeutically.

Recommendations:

1. — Because music seemed to be a contributing factor in producing regression and disturbing fantasy, its indiscriminate use should be avoided. It could be used, however, in a planned, controlled manner as a therapeutic device.

2. — Musical activities were not to be initiated until it was judged that he had gained sufficient controls over his ego not to compulsively retreat from its presentation.

3. — Music therapy was, ultimately, a treatment of choice to help improve or stabilize the regressive and unhealthy fantasies to which he retreated. It could be used to help him relate, instead, to reality, and avoid the stimulation of unhealthy fantasy.

Music Therapy

The first sessions began when Robert eagerly entered the office and immediately asked if we could hear records. He sat down, smiled and while rocking continuously, repeated his request. When asked what record he preferred, Robert answered, "Ravel's Rhaposdy Espannole."

While listening to the record, Robert displayed a consistent reaction to the music, associating it with changes in dynamics, volume, tempo. He began to masturbate, possibly indicating some deepening anxiety. He momentarily stopped masturbating and asked for a cookie. When the reply was, "I don't have any," he rocked and then asked to leave the office. No answer was forthcoming, but he made no effort to leave. Instead he remained in his chair, apparently intent again on the music. With each characteristic change in the music, he produced an associative reaction, e.g., hysterical laughter, peculiar gutteral sounds and words "nineteen fifty six" said in a sing-song tone. This he did repeatedly in the initial sessions.

Although Robert's abnormal behavior tended to be severely disturbing and disruptive to other people, he was, paradoxically, a cute and likeable boy. Using his positive personality qualities, he was able to influence most of the staff and student workers with whom he came into contact to give him cookies, apples, etc., to satisfy his seemingly incredible appetite. He would leave his scheduled activities without permission and seek out people who had fed him before in order to get more food. When this became too severe a problem, the therapist and the unit supervisor arranged that only a certain few of the staff should be allowed to feed him. They were instructed to give him treats when it seemed appropriate or rewarding to do so. Robert reacted violently to this arrangement. He threw over tables at meal times, attacked some female staff members and ran away from the unit.

During the next few sessions Robert kept talking

about going back to the hospital in which he was previously treated.

He also seemed preoccupied with the years 1953 through 1966 as they related to the model and make of certain automobiles. In most of these sessions it was his main activity. Robert seemed determined not to allow the therapist to penetrate his fantasy life. Other attempts by the therapist to break into his reveries were met with rocking, withdrawal, hysteria, etc., and on several occasions, urinating into his trousers.

Listening to records only seemed to heighten the intensity of these behavioral extremes.

The therapist discovered that Robert had his own phonograph and records given to him by his parents, and that he spent most of his time alone in his room, endlessly listening to these records. Apparently the unit staff believed this was desirable since while doing so he caused no trouble nor gave anyone any problem with discipline or control.

The therapist decided that this music in his unit room served as a harmful stimulus activating to an intense degree Robert's unhealthy fantasies, which in turn enabled him to withdraw from reality with all of its intolerable demands.

With the cooperation of the unit staff and supervisor Robert's phonograph and records were removed from his room to the therapy office. Sessions were then increased from two to five days a week, thus giving the therapist a better opportunity to observe Robert's behavior and more occasions in which to attempt to establish a relationship.

During the following sessions, the therapist began to use music as a reward for the boy's attention. Robert was told he could listen to music for one minute for every thirty seconds he occupied himself with some other directed activity such as talking or checkers. Robert persistently and mechanically asked to hear the records, but the bargain failed. Hostility and aggressiveness occurred whenever he was asked to make a decision as to what activity he would like to do. He became almost paranoid in his complaints that everyone hated him. Once his temper outburst lead him to destroy some of his beloved records. After almost all of the outbursts, he would begin to cry pathetically, possibly as a substitution for further destructive actions. This crying also looked like a manipulative maneuver to have permission to listen to records without fulfilling any of his part of the bargain. Supposedly, the therapist was to feel sorry for him. Robert subsequently chose to leave the sessions earlier than necessary when these requests were denied and he found that continued resistance on his part did not lead to the rewards he wanted.

The therapist introduced a stop watch to assist Robert in measuring his reward time. The stop watch became an effective therapeutic tool. It could be stopped whenever Robert was inattentive or fantasizing, and started again when his attention was reestablished.

After sixty sessions (over four months), the sessions began to take a positive turn due to Robert's eventual compliance with the proposed bargain. Even at this time it took him about thirty minutes to participate in an other than record listening activity for a minute and a half.

A few weeks after his indicated compliance, his attention increased to one minute, repeated five times within a thirty minute session. He was soon able to attend to the activity for a constant, unbroken five minute period, which could be repeated three times in a thirty minute period before anxiety or other disruptive elements of his behavior appeared.

He was then able to communicate verbally and nonverbally on a concious level. Compulsive rocking, exhibitionistic masturbation and destructive actions were noticably reduced.

Although this treatment seemed to be successfully reaching its goal, after two months, a sudden shift in attitude and reaction habit appeared. He began to lose the motivation of being rewarded with listening to records.

This sudden change in behavior troubled the therapist who had anticipated a breakthrough in a most difficult case. Worse, the reasons for the regression into unhealthy fantasy were unknown and unpredicted.

Upon investigation, however, it was discovered that Robert's summer counselor, had unwittingly violated the arrangement made to limit the boy's record listening only to controlled therapy sessions, and had encouraged the boy to listen to records continuously while he was with her. She believed that all children could be helped by this activity since it was supposed to relieve, encourage and comfort these 'tragic children.'

In order to regain lost ground in Robert's therapy, the therapist made special efforts to coordinate his sessions with the activities of the unit staff.

In addition a special device aimed at keeping Robert in closer touch with reality was developed. A program learning machine was connected to Robert's record player so that attending to the specially prepared program lead to music reinforcement. Music could be heard only when he pushed the proper one of three buttons for each item of the program.

The results were encouraging. Robert attended to

the task for as long as fifteen minutes, which increased to forty minutes at a time with minimal intrusion of fantasy.

Conclusion

Robert's successful treatment was accomplished through very careful observations of his behavior and cooperative team work by all staff members. While it was clear that Robert's symptomatic behavior was extremely pathological, he did show some workable assets which were the the impetus for his success in music therapy.

THE HOFFMAN TEST FOR ORGANICITY [*HTO*]

In the last chapter there were brief descriptions of the "Music Therapy Evaluation" that was administered to Mark, Joe and Robert, Since 1963, this evaluation has been used by the author in order to assess an individuals's assets and deficits and to determine the best treatment for individual problems.

It has long been the author's belief that this evaluation could be most useful in diagnosing an organic brain disorder, and, perhaps more important, could differentiate between a problem of organic brain disorder and schizophrenia. This belief stemmed from a theory that while a person with an organic brain disorder had a great deal of difficulty performing the required tasks, the schizophrenic had little difficulty, and functioned on a level much like the "normal" person.

Because the treatments for a schizophrenic and a person with organic brain disorder are totally different, it is most important that a method of differentiating the two be utilized. Until now, the differentiation has been extremely difficult, because the symptoms of the two problems often appear so similar.

After much discussion with colleagues, the author felt compelled to put this theory to the test, and in 1972 began extensive research into this area. The "Hoffman Test For Organicity" was developed from this research.

With the "Hoffman Test For Organicity", the author believes he has developed a valuable diagnostic tool to determine organicity.

It has been the author's experience that a vast number of patients displaying the symptomatic behavior of what would normally be diagnosed as schizophrenia (chronic undifferentiated type) are, in reality, exhibiting manifestations of an illness whose roots are organic in nature. We may fail to determine whether the individual is truly psychotic or is suffering from some organicity with psychotic overlays. I question how many times we are labeling patients psychotic and treating them with various modes of treatment in an attempt to bring them back to reality, when the behavior may be the result of some minimal brain damage in the receptive (sensory) or expressive (motor) areas without all of the symptomatic characteristics of aphasia, or in an area in which the damage produces inadequate integrative functions, especially in the conceptual area. Herein lies the purpose of the Hoffman Test for Organicity: 1) to determine whether or not such brain damage does exist in the patient previously diagnosed as psychotic and 2) to provide psychiatrists, psychologists and music therapists with an easily administered and valid test to differentiate between organicity and schizophrenia; 3) to provide a valid diagnostic procedure so that proper treatment could be facilitated for those found to be suffering from cerebral damage.

The following is a brief description of the research project which resulted in the formation of the Hoffman Test for Organicity.

The subjects (S's) for the research consisted of 221 individuals who were matched by age, I.Q., and by their ability to cooperate with testing procedures to understand the instructions. S's were also matched for chronicity or length of hospitilization. 63 organics, 50 schizophrenics and 108 controls (normal individuals) were chosen. All subjects in the schizophrenic and organic group had at least two diagnoses confirming their disorders. The control group consisted of randomly selected individuals who had no known neurological or psychiatric disabilities. Members of the organic group had definite diagnoses of organic brain syndrome or chronic brain syndrome. All members of the schizophrenic group had diagnoses of schizophrenic, chronic undifferentiated type, or paranoid type, with absolutely no indication of organic involvement.

Each subject was in a sound conditioned room and seated in an armless chair. Before him was placed a specially designed rhythmic apparatus. An eleven minute cassette tape recording was then used to instruct the entire test. Scoring was done concomitantly with the test.

Results

Table I shows the mean scores and standard deviations of each group in part I of the test.

TABLE I [*Part I*]

	N.	Mean	Standard Deviation
Schizophrenic	50	.5	1.22
Organic	63	4.4	3.55
Control	108	.05	.22

The brain damaged group scored on an average of 4.4; schizophrenic .5; and the control group .05.

Table II shows the mean scores and standard deviations of each group of Part II of the test.

TABLE II

	N.	Mean	Standard Deviation
Schizophrenic	50	1.38	3.27
Organic	63	25.87	13.17
Control	108	.9	2.1

The brain damaged group scored "organic" on an average of 25.87, whereas schizophrenics averaged 1.38. The control group scored an average of .9.

Table III shows the t values and their level of significance.

TABLE III

	Part I t value	Part I Level of Significance	Part II t value	Part II Level of Significance
Schizophrenic Organic	8.13	.001	14.16	.001
Schizophrenic Control	2.65	.01	.94	ns
Organic Control	31.07	.001	14.78	.001

To compute the t values, the Cochran and Cox formula was used because the population variances were unequal.
See Ferguson. Statistical Analysis in Psychology and Education. McGraw-Hill, Series in Psychology, 1966, p. 171.

On the t test on Part I, comparing the differences in mean scores for the schizophrenic and organic groups, the t value was found to be significant at .001; schizophrenic and control at .01 and organic and control at .001.

On the t test on Part II, comparing the differences in

mean scores for the schizophrenic and organic groups, the t value was found to be significant at .001; schizophrenic and control were inconsequential, and the organic and control at .001.

Discussion

The present findings show that the most accurate predictions could be found between the ages of 10.3 and 59, between organic and non-organic groups. While in Part II the performance of the organic group was significiantly higher than that of either the schizophrenic or control group, the scores of the schizophrenic and control group did not differ significantly from each other on the test. The present findings not only show that the test is a highly effective differential diagnostic tool for the organics and schizophrenics, but it hypothesised that it assesses organic dysfunctions in specific areas of the higher levels of brain function. These include auditory perception, auditory memory, and associative integration. The test also assesses fine motor coordination and the individual's basic rhythmic function. Part I of the test may prove to have some significance diagnosing all three groups.

A cross validation study is now underway. Findings of this study will be published when completed.

REFERENCES

Chapter I

Reference List

1. Lundin, Robert. an Objective Psychology of Music, 1953, p. 265
2. Ibid. p. 265
3. Meinecke, Bruno. Music and Medicine, ed. by D. Schullian & Max Schoen, (N.Y. Henry Schuman, Inc. 1948. p. 56
4. Ibid. p. 57
5. Ibid. p. 59
6. Licht, Sidney in Ludin, Robert, An Objective Psychology of Music 1953, p. 268
7. Lundin, op. cit p. 267
8. Van de Wall, Willem. Music in Hospitals, Russell Sage Foundation p. 78 1946
9. Ibid p. 38
10. Ibid. p. 41
11. Ibid. pp. 74-75
12. Ibid. pp. 75-76
13. Altshuler, Ira. Music and Medicine, Schullian & Schoen, N.Y. 1948, Ed. Henry Schuman, p. 272
14. Schneider, Erwin. An Analysis, Evaluation, and Selection of Clinical uses of Music in Therapy, 1965, Intro, p. xiv.

Chapter II

15. Schneider, Erwin. An Analysis, Evaluation, and Selection of Clinical uses of Music in Therapy, 1965, p. xiv.
16. Gaston, Thayer, Ibid. p. 3
17. Sears, William, Ibid. pp. 29-44
18. Hoffman, Norman. The Therapeutic Value of Music and It's Treatment Implications, Devereux Forum, Vol. 3, No. 1, 1966, p. 39.
19. Applebaum, Stephen. The Quest for Identity of Adjunctive Therapists, Bulletin of the Menninger Clinic, Sept. 1968, Vol. 32, No. 5., pp. 271-272

Chapter III

20. Hoffman, op. cit p. 45
21. Carmichael, L. The Onset & Early Development of behavior. In Carmichael, L (Ed.) manual of child psychology. (2nd Ed.) New York: Wiley, 1954

Gesell, A. The Embryology of Behavior, N.Y.: Harper, 1945

Hooker, D. Reflex Activities in the human fetus. In Barker, R.G., et al. (eds.) Child behavior and development. N.Y: McGraw-Hill, 1943.

Hooker, D. The prenatal origin of Behavior. Lawrence, Ks. University of Kansas Press, 1952.

Windle, W.F. Physiology of the Fetur: origin and extent of function in prenatal life. Philadelphia: Saunders, 1940.

In Thompson, George G., Child Psychology, Houghton Mifflin Co. Boston, 2nd (ed.) 1962, p. 62.

22. Sontag, L.W., & Richards, T.W. Studies in Fetal behavior: I. Fetal heart rate as a behavior indicator. Soc. Res. Child Develpm. Monogr., 1938, 3, No. 4., in Thompson op. cit. p. 67.
23. Sontag, L.W., & Wallace, R.f. Preliminary report of the Fels Fund: study of fetal activity. Amer. J. Dis. Child., 1934, 48 1050-1057., in Thompson, op. cit. p. 67.
24. Forbes, H.S., & Forbes, H. B. Fetal sense reaction: Hearing J. Comp. Psychol., 1927, 7, 353-355., in thompson, op. city. p. 68.
25. Feldman, W. M. The principles of ante-natal & post natal child psychology, pure and applied. N.Y: Longmans, 1920, in Thompson, op. cit. p. 72.
26. Spitz, Rene First Year of Life, P. 70.
27. Ibid. pp. 247-248
28. Spock, Benjamin, Baby & Child Care, 1957 Pocket Books, Inc. N.Y. p. 205.
29. Van De Wall, W. Music in Institutions, 1946, Russell Sage Foundation p. 98
30. Ibid. p. 118
31. Spitz, op. cit. pp. 243-244
32. Ibid. p. 245
33. Ibid. p. 248
34. Ibid. p. 249
35. Ibid. p. 257
36. Psychiatric Dictionary, Hinsie & Campbell, 3rd., 1960, p. 698
37. Newsweek, Reprinted from the issue of July 8, 1968. p. 47.
38. Fransella, Fay, Behav. Res. & Therapy, 1967, Vol. 5 Pergamon press Ltd. England. p. 254.
39. Taber's Cyclopedic Medical Dictionary, 10th ed. F.A. Davis Co. 1968, p. A-85.
40. Bernstein, L., The Infinite Variety of Music, Simon & Schuster, N.Y: 1966, p. 90.
41. Ibid. p. 91.
42. Ibid. p. 91.
43. Ibid. p. 95
44. Van de Wall, Op. cit., p. 57.
45. Ludin, op. cit p. 134.

Chapter 4

46. Copel, Sidney, Psychodiagnostic Study of Children and Adolescents, 1967, C.C. Thomos, pp. 91-92.
47. Rimland, Bernard. Infantile Autism, N.Y. 1964) p. 175.
48. Kanner, Leo. Autistic Disturbances of Affective Contact, **The Nervous Child**, 2 (1943), p. 217
49. Bergman, p. & Escalona, S., Unusual Sensitivities in Very Young Children, Psychoanalytic Study of the Child, 3-4 (1949), p. 334.
50. Copel, Op. City. p. 97.
51. Sherwin, A.C., Reactions to Music of Autistic (Schizophrenic) Children, American Journal of Psychiatry, May 1953, pp. 823-831.
52. Copel, S. Op. Cit. p. 101.
53. **Abnormal Psychology**, Barnes & Noble College Outline Series, No. 94, 1965, p. 146.

54. Brady, John. A Behavioral Approach to Stuttering, Pub. Paper read at the Amer. Psychiatric Ass., May 1968, p. 1-2.
55. Ibid. p. 1
56. Brady, John, A Real Rhythm Method, Newsweek, July 8, 1968, p. 47.
57. Fransella, Fay, Rhythm as a Distractor in the Modifacation of Stuttering, Behavior Res. and Therapy, 1967, Vol. 5., pp. 253-255.
58. Abnormal Psychology, Op. Cit. pp. 230-231.
59. Personal conferences, discussions, child study tapes, and observations of the work of Dr. Paul Nordoff and Clive Robbins, 1965., Philadelphia, Pa.
60. Personal Observations of a Condensed Training Workshop conducted by Ferris and Jennet Robins, Sponsored by the Devereux Foundation, Devon, Pa. Sept. 20th-24, 1965.
61. Forster, Francis, That Stardust Malady, Time, July, 1965, p. 67.
62. Abnormal Psychology., Op. Cit. p. 73.
63. Menninger, Karl., Love Against Hate, Harcourt, Brace & Co. 1942, p. 183.

Chapter 5

64. Psychiatric Dictionary, Hinsie and Campbell, Third Ed., N.Y. Oxford University Press, 1960, p. 71.
65. Altshuler, Ira M. Music and Medicine Ed. by Schullian and Schoen, by Henry Schuman, Inc. N.Y. 1948, p. 274
66. Ainlay George W. Music and Medicine, ed. by Schullian and Schoen, by Henry Schuman, Inc. N.Y. 1948, p. 326.
67. Van De Wall, Willem Music in Institutions, Russell Sage Foundation, 1936, pp. 231-232.
68. Noy, Pinchas. The Psychodynamic Meaning of Music, Journal of Music Therapy, (Dec. 1966). pp. 127-128. Vol. 3. No. 4. Part 1.
69. Ibid. Sept. 1967, Vol. 4, No. 3 Part 4. P. 84.
70. Racker, H. Contribution to Psychoanalysis of Music, Am. Imago, 1951, 8:157 (Heinrich Racker).
71. Bardas W. The Perplexities of Music, Imago, 1919, 5:364-371 Teller, Frieda. Musikegnuss and Pahntasie. Imago, 1917, 5:8-15 Alvin, Juliette. Music for the Handicapped Child, 1965, p. 100 Germaine, A.G., Musik und das Ubewusste, Int. Ztschr. Psychoanal., 1928, 14:568.

Van Den Daele, Leland. A Music Projective Technique, Journal of Projective Techniques and Personality assessment, Vol. 31, No. 5. 1967, pp. 48-49.